and Peace :)
-Diana Douglas

The Book of Wonders

Diana Douglas

Cover Artwork by

Katie Goodwill

Dedicated to my best friend Owen Norris and his family. Thank you for everything, and for showing me what a best friend really is.

List of Poems

Prologue: Life

What exactly does life mean to you? As you read this piece, please contemplate your answer to this question.

Life is full of ups and downs. How do you deal with life when times get rough? Without the tough times, the good times would not be as meaningful. Accept life for what it is and make the most out of every day. There are 24 hours in a day. How will you spend your day?

When life gets tough it can be hard to keep going. You know what though? You can get through anything you put your mind to! You may ask, but how will I get through this? There are many ways to get through these tough times.

One way to get through these tough times or struggles in life is to find one positive thing in every situation. Finding a positive can help you see the problem easier, which will help you figure out how to deal with it. No matter how hard, identifying a positive can help you stay strong during this tough time.

A second way to get through tough times is to make sure you save a half hour to an hour for something you enjoy doing. Your happiness is important, so every day make sure you do at least one thing that will make you happy. When you do something that makes you happy it will help you to access the tough time clearly with an open mind. Doing this will also relax you, and it will most likely make the situation at least a little easier.

A third way to get through these tough times is to have at least one or two people that you can talk to. I know it can be hard to trust people, but try to have a few people you can tell anything to. Keeping your feelings bottled up inside is not healthy. If you haven't found two people you trust, at least try to have one. Having at least one person you can tell anything and everything to will give you a chance to vent, get advice, and extra comfort. Trust is something that is earned and not just given, so I know it takes time to trust someone. Have hope, everything will be okay!

There are so many ways to get through the difficult times in life. When life's got you down, find at least two or three things that will help you get through it best. No two people are the same. No one can do you better than you. You matter! Please try to stay strong. You can not have a rainbow without having sunshine and rain. It may be rainy now but it won't rain forever. The sun will soon shine!

There are seven days in a week. It is absolutely okay to have tough days! On difficult days though try to have hope. If you are having a tough day, I hope that tomorrow is a better day for you. Even if it's a tough day today, make the most out of the day. Tomorrow is not necessarily promised, and it's a mystery. Yesterday is now history. Live for today, no matter what you're going through!

This piece is coming to a close. Here are a few questions I want to leave you with. What exactly does life mean to you? Everyone leaves a mark or impact on the world. What mark will you leave? How do you want to be remembered? Please be positive and make the most out of every day! Try to smile, and live life to the fullest. Don't take life for granted.

Part One

Who Are You???

Reader,
Even the strongest
heart-needs protecting
Do you want to go??
A million miles-be there
Make your mark
Where the free luxury is offered
Be free
Be you
Stay true
Don't change for someone else
Only change for yourself
Treasure your family
Treasure your friends
Be the light across the world
Life is too short-
To live with regrets
Go out-
Make your mark.

The Music Box

Small notes of music are heard,
From somewhere far away...
While the sound occasionally lingers,
Fairly close to a set of ears.

There is something called a music box,
And it plays a masterpiece...
For anyone willing to listen,
To the message hidden inside.

When the box is wound by you or me,
The symphony begins trying to tell...
Each man and woman that may be listening,
Something heartfelt.

Each music box has a different story to tell,
For they were all created...
With someone special in mind,
So each music box ends up unique.

When the music seems far away,
It's almost like a message in a bottle...
Waiting to be read by caring heart,
But in reality it just wants to be heard...
Instead of being silenced,
By a cold heart of stone.

When the music begins to linger,
Near a pair of listening ears...
Every emotion can be felt,
For music box's hide nothing in their song.

If you close your eyes someday,
After winding a music box...
Listen closely to the tune,
And try to feel the message...
That it's trying to tell you,
And find comfort in the fact...
That you're as special as a music box,
Because the Heavenly Father...
Gave us all a heartbeat and breath in our lungs...
Which is like the music,
Of your music box.

A Genuine I Love You

There's at least a million ways,
For someone to say...
I love you.
There's at least a million ways...
For someone to show someone,
That when they say I love you...
They really truly mean it.

I love you looks different,
Coming from each person...
But when it's genuine and real,
It's beautiful and irreplaceable.
You don't have to say the words,
I love you...
For it's possible for someone to know,
Through other phrases and your actions.

I love you can sound like-
Put your seatbelt on,
Or
Drive safely...
And let me know when you land.

I love you can sound like-
Drink plenty of water,
And eat something...
For I want you to be well nourished.

I love you can look like-
Time spent together,
Or
Thoughtful gestures...
Like a gift that says,
I saw this and thought of you.

I love you can look like-
A hug or a kiss,
Reminding the person...
That they're forever valued.

I love you can be used-
For family and friends...
Or
For the person who's your soulmate.

I love you can be used-
In so many ways...
But in today's world,
So many people throw it away.
When I say I love you,
I mean it with everything I am...
And if more people did that,
Less people would be broken-hearted.

Not Knowing Where to Start

The people of the world may hear your heart,
Along with occasional cries for help...
But that doesn't mean they'll do their part,
To help keep your heart from falling apart...
For not everyone knows where to start,
When trying to find and protect...
Someone else's happiness,
Especially since melancholy feelings...
Are much easier to locate in this day and age.

The Warm and Comforted Heart

The moon heard the woman's cries,
Which caused the stars to say Goodbye..
Since apparently the sunshine,
Needed to warm her heart with comfort...
Before darkness could encompass her,
Without fully hurting her...
Since starlight will never compare,
To the sunlight and it's warmth.

The Turned Cheek

The poet sews together the words,
That the heart bleeds out...
For this world is a harsh place,
That's full of melancholy...
Hunting for a smile or laugh,
As very few souls...
Realize how valuable,
A kind helping hand is...
For most just turn their cheek,
When someone's in need.

The Remaining Heartbeat

When I smile...
What do you see?

When I laugh...
What do you hear?

When I cry...
What do you feel?

If you honestly care,
As much as you say you do...
Then please show it,
Before it's too late.

Life is far from an easy battle...
But with God on my side - I'll be okay.

My tears won't last forever...
But then again - neither will my smile.

My laughter may fade away,
But my heartbeat will remain the same.

The Speechless Raindrop

The sound of rain is soothing,
While the sight of rain leaves me speechless...
For the raindrops that fall,
Never reveal where they're headed.

The sun that shines- is so bright sometimes,
That I need to find someplace to hide...
In order to protect my eyes from a lifetime,
Of damage that hurts within as well...
For I wish to someday have children,
And watch them grow up even though...
I won't know where they'll be headed,
Just like the sun that warms the earth...
Has stopped me from watching its journey.

When the sun goes down- late at night,
The moon and stars come out...
Lighting the way for dreams to come true-
Which means that the pathway to forever,
Is now able to be clearly seen...
For the Lord is showing the world,
That no matter what happens in life...
It'll always be you and me conquering it.
The sound of rain is soothing,
While the sight of rain leaves me speechless...
For the raindrops that fall,
Never reveal where they're headed.
The days of the week have taught me,
A great deal of things about my past...
Which in essence will make my future,
Twice as beautiful- since I also try...
To live in the moment when I feel it's safe.

The clock that seems to never stop ticking,
Is doing an accurate job of keeping track...
Of something that's called time,
And time is a tricky thing...
For people like me- never know how much,
Is given to them for living...
And time never lets anyone see,
When it'll stop- causing everything to freeze...
Which is why it's critical to value each moment alive,
For anyone's heartbeat clock could stop...
At any time without warning,
Not letting us see them off to Heaven properly.

The sound of rain is soothing,
While the sight of rain has left me speechless...
For the raindrops that fall...
Never reveal where they're headed,
But I know that within each raindrop...
Are tears sent from loved ones in Heaven.

The Clock's Heartbeat

The heart is a clock,
For each heart beat...
It's ticking away,
Counting down...
Each moment in time.

The clock goes ticktock,
Just like the heart goes boom...

As time fades into memories,
It challenges each man and woman...
To reflect on the life they live,
While living in the moment...
Instead of fretting about the future,
That's not even in reach.

Life is a riddle that's waiting,
To be solved daily...
Which is why the clock and the heart,
Play such a vital role...
In this mysterious place called Earth,
Until all the people of the world...
Hear the Lord's voice,
Calling them to their Heavenly Home.

Guarded Treasure

If you don't treasure your woman,
Let her go - someone else will.

If you don't love your woman,
Let her go - she'll be worth the world...
To someone else.

Just remember one thing,
If you push her away...
She'll be gone for good,
Never giving you - another chance.

If you treat her love as a joke,
Step aside - for an honest lover...
Would take her seriously.

If you don't love or treasure your woman,
Then tell me - why is she yours?

The Hidden Scream

She won't scream her needs,
Out-loud for everyone to hear...
Since she's as independent as can be.

The woman you see in front of you,
Could be in a state of melancholy...
Without ever alerting you.

So if you claim to love the woman,
Standing in front of you...
Look her in the eyes - for they'll reveal,
Whatever her smile won't.

The woman in front of you,
Can be a mystery at times...
But show her you care.

She won't scream her needs,
Out-loud for everyone to hear...
So pay attention while she's with you.

The Missing Magnetic Pull

If you push her away,
Don’t expect her to come back.

People can only handle,
So much neglect...
Before they say I’m done,
And then move on.

If you push her away,
You most likely...
Won’t see her again,
So don’t get your hopes up.

Think long and hard before you push,
Your woman away...
And if you wouldn’t miss her,
Then please let her try to find true love.

If you push her away,
Don’t expect her to come back.

The Tales That Fill My Lungs

The tales about young men,
Tend to end tragically...

The tales about young women,
Tend to be quite complicated...

The tales about life and death,
Fill my lungs - revealing new facts...
With each passing day.

The tales that speak about dreams,
Don't reveal what wants to be seen...
Since humans are greedy and need grace.

The tales that speak of history,
Remind folks life is but a mystery...

The tales that speak of futures unseen,
Remind you and me to just breathe.

The Last Lovely Dance

When love is 100% true,
It'll be as beautiful as a ballerina…
Dancing her last dance,
For there's nothing to hide.

When love is 100% Pure,
There will be no room for doubt…
For an honest love,
Has zero room for secrets.

A love that's breathtaking and real,
Is hard to find now-a-days…
Since so many people are greedy,
While not caring about their victims.

Be careful when letting your walls down,
Please pray and trust your gut…
About who you should lower them for,
After all - you only deserve the best

If you're someone who's blessed,
To have found their soulmate…
Cherish and treasure them,
For a bond like that in today's world…
Is almost completely extinct.

The Confession

When you whispered my name,
Telling me that you loved me…
My heart dropped,
Asking you to Prove it.

As a Person who got used to,
Being taken advantage of…
Constantly getting hurt,
My heart put up a wall…
To Protect itself,
And to see if anyone was worth it.

When you held me close,
Our hearts filled each others…
Missing beats - creating a harmony,
That's so rare but beautiful.

The next time you confessed,
Telling me you love me…
I smiled back and said,
I love you too - giving you all of me…
Please be careful with this life of mine,
For my heart and soul are still fragile.

The War Zone

The never ending war…
Isn't just inside.

The never ending war,
That the Enemy started…
Destroyed everything around me,
Before trying to burn me alive.

The never ending war,
That the Enemy started…
Is one that has taught me a lot,
Especially about people I can trust.

The never ending war,
Has been terrible…
But when I called upon the Lord,
He saved me-showing this Child of his…
That the enemy was not going to win,
No matter how hard he tried.

We the people-all have scars…
Each one with a backstory,
Explaining their presence…
But we must remember,
That through God our Father…
We will be victorious,
Even with the Enemy's attacks.

The never ending war,
Yearns to hear Hallelujah

The Double Edge Sword

I'm tired of getting hurt by people…
God-I know you have a plan,
For my life and will never…
Abandon me on my journey.

Lately I have been far from okay…
And wouldn't mind seeing the blueprint,
Or map you drew up…
For this Earthly life of mine.

I'll rejoice when you take me home,
Away from this harsh-melancholy world...
That tries to drown me,
And make me question your promises.

I try to sing hallelujah…
In the valleys and mountains,
But sometimes my praise gets muffled…
For the Enemy tries to lead me away from you.

Since life has been so crazy later…
I want to make sure-I set aside time,
To give thanks for all of life's adventures…
And to remember you'll always be with me.

Eyes

The eyes of my past,
Point and laugh...
At the new me.

The eyes of my past,
Tell me what won't last...
For I've dealt with lots of burdens.

The eyes of my future,
Sometimes tell me...
The things I wanna hear.

The eyes of my future,
Strongly encourage me...
To treasure the present.

My eyes are quite powerful,
In the realm...
Of the past, present, and future.

My eyes are quite powerful,
For they're fixed on God's word...
Since he truly knows best.

What Should I Do?

Why do you enjoy my tears?

Why do you want my anxieties...
To scream so loud everyone hears?

My exhausted heart calls out,
God- when will you take me home?
I just wanna walk by your side.

This world you brought me into,
Is beyond cruel and hateful...

What should I do? Please help me Lord.

Real

I just want something real,
Similar to a breath of fresh air...

Is that too much to ask for,
In this harsh greedy world?

I'm tired of fighting...
So it's a good thing that God,
Will win the battle I'm in.

My armor of God is on...
So the enemy can't trick me,
Into believing his lies.

It'll be nice to someday join the Lord,
At his heavenly throne when my time comes.

I just want something real,
Why is that too crazy to ask for?

The Realities of Humanity

I'm not a video game,
Or a board game...
So please don't play me.

I'm human just like you,
But I value honesty...
So please respect that.

I'm not a video game,
Or a board game...
But I am a child of God.

I may have flaws,
But everyone does...
It's a reality of humanity.

I'm not a video game,
Or a board game....
So please don't treat me like I am.

Avoiding A Road of Trouble

If you're with someone,
And you genuinely...
Don't wanna lose them,
Make it known...
To where it's hard to forget.

If you're with someone,
And you don't want them...
To distance themselves,
Then make sure they know...
How closely you wanna hold them.

If you're with someone,
Know that effort...
Is a two way street,
And not a one way road...
Otherwise there can be trouble.

If you're with someone,
Make sure they know...
How you truly feel,
This way if tomorrow,
Doesn't come...
It won't be too late.

The Burnt Bridge

Don't tell me that you cared...
You fooled me once,
And I'm not going down that road again.

I know now the game you were playing,
For most guys have a habit of doing it...
You just wanted someone to boost your ego,
But I value honesty and trust along with loyalty.

Now that you screwed me over,
I'll forgive you for what you did...
But I'm not returning to a toxic relationship,
I'm not a punching bag to be used.

You may claim you cared,
But if you did your actions...
Would have proved it,
So please don't waste your time...
Telling me you'll always care,
For you've already burned the bridge...
Of me ever believing a single word,
That ever comes out of your mouth.

The Lady that Never Returned

One day you'll see someone,
Steal the tears that you put in her eyes…
And replace them with a happier gleam.

If you expect her to stay,
Depressed forever…
When you broke her heart,
You're out of luck.

There are people that love,
The woman you tore apart…
And almost destroyed.

If you expect the woman,
That you claimed to love…
To never move on after your games,
You're out of luck - she deserves to smile.

One day you'll see someone,
Making the woman who gave you…
Her whole heart - happy like you once did.

So if you're pushing your woman away,
Make sure it's what you truly want…
For once she's gone - she'll forever disappear.

The Final Word

When you pushed me away,
It was like daggers attacked...
My body, heart, soul, mind, and lungs,
But you don't care cause your ego...
Started getting hurt since it couldn't handle,
Being real & honest & loyal for once.

When you pushed me away,
I was hesitant to give up on you...
For I take all my relationships seriously -
Whether it be a friendship,
A family thing...
Or the one where I find my soulmate,
For I value honesty & loyalty more than most.

Now that I've walked away and let go,
Since you decided to push me away...
I hope you understand the fact,
That I'm gone for good...
You had your chance and you blew it,
For I know my worth in God's eyes...
And you were treating me like dirt,
Even though I failed to see it at first.

This is my final word to you,
So if you're reading this...
It's too late to change things,
So don't waste your time...
Trying to fix what can't be fixed,
Goodbye - have a nice life.

The Broken Vows

You have broken your vows to me,
Along with the biggest promise...
That you've ever made in your life.

When you decided to crush,
The beautiful thing we had...
My Heavenly Father saw my pain,
And lead my heart, soul, body, and mind...
To a guy that honestly values me,
Because the Lord realized...
That your desperate lying self,
Was being held by the enemy...
Who was making sure that you,
Never genuinely loved me...
For he loves to watch people suffer,
Especially anyone that's valuable to God.

Now that your vows have been broken,
Don't come crawling back to me...
Because I'll never let you near me again.

The Poisoned Evening

When you took her on a Picnic,
She was nothing but a witness…
To your evil and cruel heart,
For you only offered her poison…
Without batting an eye,
While laughing.

When you destroyed her heart,
You wondered why…
People stopped checking in,
So you began to realize…
That she was the main one,
Who noticed your silence.

I hope you've now learned,
That if someone genuinely…
Loves you for you,
They'll notice your lack of words…
And they'll go out of their way,
To show you how important you are.

She loved you with all she had,
While you practically executed her…
Proudly showing blood,
All over your hands…
Excited that you made the world,
A little darker than before…
Since her light was dimmed,
By an unknown enemy…
Who just wanted everyone,
To feel the pain life threw his way.

The Gift of Pain

Your hurtful words wounded,
A heart as precious as gold…
The one you claimed to love.

Why gift someone pain,
After they've done nothing…
Except try to be what you needed?

Why gift someone Pain,
When they only wanted…
What was best for you?

Your hurtful words,
May cause wounds…
But they'll never kill -
So don't build your ego too high.

You've gifted pain to many folks,
And several wonder why…
Or what they did wrong.

You think you have won…
but, each soul that you made grieve -
Will move on and laugh again…
Even if it kills you to see,
Each person happy again.

No one that you hurt will ever,
Stay down or depressed…
So think twice before,
You hurt another person -
Please just always be honest and kind.

Peace Turned to War

True love is almost extinct.

People these days…
Would rather stab their loved one,
Either in the heart or back.

Peace is hard to find.

People these days…
Would rather have a war,
Not caring who gets wounded or hurt.

Being born in the wrong time,
Is beyond difficult…

Especially since it's easy,
To wish God would call you to Heaven…
Away from all of the hatred and stupidity,
For honest love and peace is all you want.

Before jumping to conclusions,
Say a prayer - and trust your gut…
Since the Lord would never,
Lead you astray.

Till Death Do Us Part

Her happily ever after,
Will not be with…
Who the world tries,
To force upon her!

Her happily ever after,
Will not be with …
Someone who is abusive,
Mentally or physically.

Her happily ever after,
Is something that's between…
God and the woman,
Who is mentioned in this poem.

Happily ever after will look,
Different in everyone's book…
But we mustn't hate or gawk,
On couples that are in love.

Happily ever after,
Is a beautiful thing - but…
So many folks throw it away,
Because the water got rough momentarily.

Happily ever after,
Is something that everyone…
Deserves to have in life,
For no one deserves to die alone.

If you're not pleased with life,
Pray about it - and take action…
Since change won't happen,
If you neglect hard work/effort.

The Lover's Request

Don't tell me you love me,
If you don't plan to show it.

Don't tell me you love me one day,
And then turn around the next...
With a changed mind.

If you can't be genuine and real,
Then why even bother...
Holding me near?

Don't tell me you love me,
If it's far from the truth.

Don't tell me you love me,
Unless your heart means it 100%.

The Erased Love Story

Is it so wrong for a woman,
To want to be genuinely loved?

Instead of being the person,
That's easily replaced…
Or forgotten about?

Instead of being the burden to people,
And getting told she's better off…
Dead instead of alive?

Women may be fragile creatures,
But they're stronger than most think…

Especially since a lot of people
Would rather see them suffer…
In melancholy feelings,
Without a trace of happiness.

All women are different but beautiful,
Even though society tries to say otherwise…

This world we live in doesn't care,
About the human heart and soul…
Mainly just the body - sometimes the mind.

Why is it so scary or wrong, or stupid,
For a woman to want a happily ever after?

Protection

There is a huge difference,
Between love and lust…

Love is pure and kind,
While lust is greedy…
And sometimes hurtful.

Love is brutally honest,
While lust oftentimes…
Makes people feel ashamed,
In some way shape or form.

There is a huge difference,
Between love and lust…

Love that lasts forever,
Is truly hard to find…
But it can be found,
Because oftentimes…
It hunts down people,
That have stopped searching.

Love comes in all shapes and sizes,
While being seen in many forms…
Like a lot of friendships,
Or when someone finds their soulmate.

There is a huge difference,
Between love and lust…

Lust is a scary thing,
Since it doesn't always care…
Who it tears apart,
As long as it gets what it wants.

Lust often has a fairly large ego,
So please be careful…
And protect your heart, soul, body and mind.

There is a huge difference,
Between love and lust…
But many somehow manage
To always confuse the two.

Inseparable Hearts

Your eyes have met mine...
So please don't waste my time -
I want us to last a lifetime,
Even if in the meantime...
Some folks get upset.

Not everyone will understand,
A love so divine like ours....
One that makes goodbyes hard,
Where we hate being apart...
At least for very long,
For our hears have always been one...
Making us inseparable.

If anyone wishes to tear us apart,
They'll be unsuccessful...
For they'd have to go through,
The Heavenly Father...
The one who brought us together,
Turning two individuals - into one.

We'll always have ups and downs,
But there is no one in the world...
I'd rather conquer life with,
Than you sweetheart...
For you're my one and only.

One and Only

I lay awake thinking of you,
You're always on my mind.
Forever may be a long time,
But even eternity with you-
Won't be enough time.
You're my one and only,
We're soulmates.

I used to try to find love,
Forgetting what God told me-
Then when I gave up...
Then suddenly it was clear
That he gave me you,
I just truly never opened my eyes.

With you time stops,
A promise of love-
A love so true,
Even the blind know it's real.

I lay awake thinking of you,
You're always on my mind.
Forever may be a long time,
But even eternity with you-
Won't be enough time.
You're my one and only,
We're soulmates.

I ask for forever,
I ask for always-
To be by your side.
Without you,
Each breaths-
A struggle.

You're my forever,
And I'm your always.

God taught me,
Right from wrong-
Everything with you
Is perfect.
I thank God all the time,
For blessing me with you.

I lay awake thinking of you,
You're always on my mind.
Forever may be a long time,
But even eternity with you-
Won't be enough time.
You're my one and only,
We're soulmates-
And with you I am…
Truly home.

The Beautiful Testimony

The woman's fragile heart,
Was ruined by sunlight...
But rescued by starlight,
When things with her world...
Were far from right.

In the blink of an eye she asked God why,
And while waiting for the Lord's reply...
Her better half came by to check on her,
For he loves & misses her - & worries bout her.
More than he may care to admit,
But the man & woman...
Conquer everything together.

The woman's fragile heart,
Has been through great pain...
But the pain created scars,
That may sometimes be painful...
Since they're creating a beautiful testimony,
That shows how the Heavenly Father...
Never abandons his children.

Love

What is love?
Love is pure,
Love is a cure.
There is more-
To a heart.
Hearts do more,
Than pump blood.
Hearts do more,
Than give us life.
What is love?
Love shows us,
We are not alone-
Love shows us,
We are cared for.
Why hate,
When you can love?
Why hate,
When you can be kind?
Actions,
Are louder-
Than words.
Go out-
Make your mark,
On the world.
One person-
Can make a difference.
What is love?
What will your mark be?
Love is slowly changing,
The world.
Have hope-
What is love?

Happiness

Smile.
Laugh.
Love.
Be kind.
Live life fully-
No time for regrets...
Make your mark on the world
True happiness??
People can make you happy-
Things can make you happy-
You decide what makes you happy...
When things get rough, don't give up
Keep your head up- stay strong
You can't make a rainbow- without rain AND sunshine
So...
Smile,
and
Laugh.
Live,
and
Love.
Stay strong,
and
Never quit.

Everywhere I Turn

Everywhere I turn it seems like,
Someone's either getting married...
Or having a baby.

Everywhere I turn it seems like,
The other people around me...
Have a higher chance of success.

Everywhere I turn it seems like,
No one knows how to be real anymore...
For they all seem fake and dishonest.

Everywhere I turn it seems like,
This world only gets more dangerous...
Since people have lost sight of the Lord.

Everywhere I turn - there happens to be,
Melancholy feelings mixed with anger...
And a hint of happiness.

Everywhere I turn it seems like,
The Enemy is trying to drown...
God's precious children.

I'll never understand why,
Life has to be extremely challenging...
But I'm thankful for each day I'm alive.

The Daggers Thrown at Women

We live in a harsh judgemental world,
One that tries to tell women…
What they "have" to look like,
In order to actually be beautiful.

It's almost like us ladies,
Need permission or something…
To be who we wanna be,
Without getting torn apart.

We may have people that want us,
Dead or alive - or somewhere, in between…
This is where we need to take a stand,
It's time that we're finally heard.

ALL sizes are beautiful,
ALL shapes are beautiful…
ALL of YOU is beautiful,
It's time to turn down the volume…
Of the harsh judgmental world,
For we were all born to be different.

If God wanted us ladies to ALL look the same,
Then he would have designed us that way…
But when the Enemy tries to convince us,
We're not beautiful - we need to ignore him.

Whether we meet in person or not,
As a woman I stand with you…
And remind you that it is possible,
To get through all of life's challenges.

Strength Over Weakness

You may want to see me suffer,
BUT…
I'll smile and look you in the eyes,
For no one will ever be able to…
Rob me of true peace and happiness-

God…
Won't let them be taken from me,
For even though I know pain…
Along with melancholy feelings,
He reminds me that no matter what…
Life is worth living and experiencing-

Especially…
With the Lord forever by my side.
The devil may want you to believe,
That you will be able to help destroy me…
But you couldn't be more wrong-

Because…
God will always Protect his children.
Thank you for helping me become,
Stronger in my faith.

The Love of Paparazzi

The beauty that shines within,
Is what the Paparazzi should love…

Looks will fade and run away,
So the camera's should only…
Be capturing the beauty,
That a moment holds.

The beauty of a moment,
Can last forever with a Photo…
But often times the People,
Weren't worried about how they looked.

If you truly want to be seen,
Especially in today's world…
Have a beautiful heart, soul and mind,
Because then you'll become a legend.

True beauty comes from within,
So ignore the drama searching paparazzi.

When you're old and gray –
You'll be glad,
That you followed your heart…
Instead of listening to the media.

The Sun Shines – Even when it Rains

If you want ot be with someone,
Who has a heart of gold…
And is a rare soul,
You'll have to accept the fact…
That you'll have walls to climb,
For she's been hurt before.

The person that you can't,
Seem to get off your mind…
Has a soul made of glass,
So when you go to admire…
Handle with care,
Or you may never get a chance…
To love and appreciate,
Whomever you've fallen for.

If someone is special to you,
Make it known…
So they never go to sleep,
Wondering if they matter…
And if the world would notice,
Their absence some day.

Take a chance and let your voice,
Be truly heard and acknowledged…
For true love still exists,
You just have to be willing…
To fight for it daily,
Instead of giving up in rough waters.

More

We started,
As friends.
We slowly grew-
Into way more.
You're my man,
I'm your girl.
I trust you,
With all of me.
A hug,
Leads
To a kiss.
Your embrace-
Is comforting.
Your arms,
Are more to me,
Than just arms.
They are my home.
You mean more to me,
Than you know.
I hope you're aware-
Of how special you are.
I love you.
My heart,
Is yours.
You are more,
Than you think.
You are a dream,
One that's come true.
I'm thankful,
And blessed.
You are more,
Than my man,
You're my heart's song.

Him

Smiles,
Laughter,
Memories-
Never getting tired,
Of him.
Good morning,
Good evening,
I know he cares.
Love at first sight?
Arms that feel like home.
I knew,
He had my heart-
From that very first moment,
He's been careful,
With my heart.
Our hearts,
Have blossomed-
Into one.
I love him so much!

Soulmates

I look at you,
I talk with you,
I soar high above-
The clouds.
We're soulmates.
I didn't really know,
Where home was-
But all along,
It was in your arms.
Your loving embrace,
Makes me feel wanted.
You make me soar,
High above the clouds.
You're a dream come true,
I know true love exists-
Thanks to you.
Soulmates-
Go through good times,
And bad times,
Which makes their love grow.
Love blossoms,
Like a flower that doesn't die.
You're my soulmate-
I hope to spend forever,
With you by my side.

YOU

Your eyes are the ocean-
Your smile is the sunrise & sunset.
Your heart is pure,
Our love story-
So special and beautiful.
I never knew,
Love could be-
This pure and true,
Until you came along.
You mean more to me,
Than words or actions-
Could ever prove.

The Anniversary

Date one lead to date two,
Along with the many more...
That has led to forever.

You stole my heart,
Straight from the beginning...
When God gave me you,
And each moment we're together...
Will always be treasured,
For you're the love of my life.

As we celebrate our anniversary,
Let's take a moment...
To embrace each other,
For OUR special day is finally here.

Our ups and downs,
Our strengths and weaknesses...
Make us stronger as one.

Whether we're sick or healthy,
Whether we're rich or poor...
We'll get through it all together,
With the Lord cheering us on.

I could get extra emotional,
And make this poem extremely long...
But I just want to say,
Happy Anniversary...
I love you to infinity and beyond!

Love In Full Bloom

As I hear the birds sing early in the morning,
It makes me think of you and me...
And all of our memories,
For you're the one who makes life complete.

As the birds sing their wonderful tune,
Breakfast cooks in the oven...
Making a smell that permeates the kitchen,
Giving everyone's nose in the house...
A whiff of what was to come,
For when breakfast was finished being made.

As family gathers around the table,
To finally eat together...
Hands are held and grace is given,
Then shortly afterwards...
The tastebuds become satisfied,
For they're blessed to have food on the table.

After the start of the day,
Things become a little more fast paced...
For there are only so many hours,
In each day that the Lord has made.

Once the day is done it becomes easy to see,
Just how busy life can truly be...
And why it's beyond worth it,
To have rest days.
If we're not super careful,
Then some of life's treasures...
Will pass us by,
In the blink of an eye.

Together as one we can make it through anything,
Beautiful or difficult for the Lord is on our side.

As time continues to go on,
Our love continues to blossom...
For true love never dies,
It only blossoms and grows...
And the Heavenly Father...
Has blessed us with each other.

The Test of Time

Nighttime showers try to drown all the flowers,
While making as many people as possible...
Suffer a great deal of pain.

The morning sunrise takes a look at you and I,
Then grabs a hand of yours & a hand of mine...
For the Lord knows we'll stand the test of time.

God has given me you,
For the beautiful and difficult times...
That life will offer us.

The world continues to spin round and round,
But more and more hate has filled the place...
Making Earth truly heartbreaking.

God has given me you,
For the beautiful and difficult times...
That life will offer us.

The Heavenly Father has given us,
All a name and a purpose...
We just have to trust his plan.

God has given me you,
For the beautiful and difficult times...
That life will offer us.

Not having a blueprint or photo,
For what each individual day should look like...
Can make things challenging for everyone.

Whenever we the people,
Feel lost & alone or afraid & helpless...
The Lord does everything he can,
To reassure us no harm will come to us tonight.

God has given me you,
For the beautiful and difficult times...
That life will offer us.

As the past is forever remembered,
And the present is forever treasured...
The future must be prepared for,
This way history won't repeat itself.

Time

Clocks ticking-
Minute by minute,
Second by second.
Hours and days,
Weeks and months,
Don't forget years-
All go by.
Time stands still,
Time moves quickly.
Memories etched,
Into brains and hearts.
Time is everlasting-
Go out,
Make your mark.

Family and Friends

Houses,
Streets-
Love.
Family,
Not always blood-
Friends,
Sometimes related.
Home is more,
Than a house.
Hearts love,
Unconditionally.
Family and friends,
Life matters.
Memories-
With family,
And friends,
Treasure all times.

Hourglass

One breath at a time,
Each life an hourglass-
Time running out.
An hourglass heartbeat,
Time is precious.
Tombstones have a dash.
How will you,
Be remembered?
Life is an hourglass,
The final breath arrives-
It's time to leave,
Your legacy lives on.

Roses

Flower petals,
Form a rose-
Roses are white,
Blue and red.
Roses are pink,
Yellow and purple-
Each rose is different,
No two the same.
Petals fall eventually.
The rose remains,
Beautiful!

The Echoing Tears

My heart and soul have been left to cry alone.

Each tear that's shed echos into the void,
Of what's meant to be the future...

I'm aware of my past and the history,
That I wish to make sure...
Never repeats.

I am aware of my present for the daily pains,
Just refuse to go away...
But hey - miracles happen everyday.
I am aware that everyone has a future,
But at this exact moment...
I'm not sure how bright mine will be.

My heart and soul have been left to cry alone.

Each tear that's shed echos into the void,
Of what's meant to be the future...
So as I accept the challenge,
Of living another day...
I hunt for reasons to smile,
Because I'm tired of always hurting.

I accept the fact that life on Earth is short,
And that life in Heaven with the Lord...
Is one where everyone belongs-
People just have to believe...
Along with allowing God to guide them,
For he's the only one who makes us victorious.

As I complete my daily tasks or chores,
I make sure that my actions...
Are a reflection of things I've said,
For I want them to match one another.

Actions are the echo to someone's words,
And I'll always do my absolute best...
To make sure they go hand in hand,
Never straying from one another.

My heart and soul have been left to cry alone.

Each tear that's shed echos into the void,
Of what's meant to be the future...
And as I try to dream of what could be,
My past haunts me...
Affirming that I'm an easy target,
For I'm just a woman...
That's been neglected and hurt,
In more ways than anyone should.

My heart and soul have been left to cry alone.

Each tear that's shed echoes into the void,
Of what's meant to be the future...
And my guardian angels,
Will forever be a part of me...
No matter what anyone says,
For their love and legacy left behind...
Are attached and anchored in place,
In the memory box that my heart and soul...
Are very protective of.

Old memories and new memories,
Both are treasured...
But some are still being created,
For I've found my one true love...
Since the Lord gave me his hand,
And I will protect him no matter what...
For I am attached to my one and only.

To the man that has all of me...
I hope you never get tired,
Of hearing the phrase “I do”...
For I’ll never stop reminding you,
Of how proud I am of you...
Along with how honored I am,
That you made me yours.

At one point and time,
My heart and soul had been left...
To cry alone.

Each tear that was shed echoed into the void,
Of what was meant to be the future...
Then my Heavenly Father called my name,
Holding out his hand to help guide me...
And when I took his hand I was weak,
But he has given me strength...
To conquer everyday alive,
Even on the ones where hiding...
Seems like the best option,
I refuse to give up on the life I was given.

Yearning for A Better World

My heart feels dark since love is forever underrated.

My heart is bleeding - wondering if violence ever end...

My heart feels blue since the world is disappointing.

My heart tries to see the bright side of things - So Heaven, please be near...

My heart is broken, so it wonders when I'll happily dance.

My heart is heavy since every day seems to be never ending.

My heart feels dark since the world is cruel, so I'm ready to go home...

My heart feels blue since life is extremely tiring.

My heart is bleeding - But I'm trying to smile.

My heart is heavy since it knows history is always in the making...

My heart feels dark since hatred seems to get more attention that love.

My bleeding heart feels compassion for this cruel world.

My heart is heavy since it just wants to make the world a better home.

Will you join me in making the world we live in - a better place?

Holidays

Home,
Or far away-
Holidays mean more,
Than location.
Make do,
With what you have.
Celebrate,
With family and friends.
Holidays,
Mean more-
Than parties.
Holidays,
Are reminders,
To not take life-
For granted.
YOU truly matter,
Happy holidays!

Thanksgiving

Family,
Friends-
Or time alone,
It's thanksgiving.
The year has flown!
Remember-
To be thankful.
Always give thanks,
Not just on Thanksgiving.
Memories,
Good or bad-
Always be thankful,
No matter what.
Live life to the fullest,
For God is good!

Birthdays

Childhood,
Adulthood-
People grow.
Birthdays,
Every year-
Let's celebrate.
Birthdays and reflections,
Time flies!
Maturity,
Doesn't come from age.
Whether it's your birthday,
Or not-
Consider this,
A reminder.
YOU MATTER!
Let your light shine.

Raise A Glass for Therapy

Prayer, Music, and Poetry...
Are beautiful forms of therapy,
So I hope you'll join me...
In raising a glass for a toast,
About never giving up...
And learning to pray more,
Even when words are hard to find...
For our heart, soul, mind, and body,
Have been through a lot of trauma...
But the pain that we've been through,
Doesn't mean we're unloved...
Because God loves ALL of his children,
And with him everything is possible...
Even though at times it's hard,
To comprehend why or how...
Some things happen(ed) in life.

I'm proud of how far you've come,
So hold on a little longer because miracles...
Usually happen when they're least expected.
You and your life matter...
And I hope you won't forget that.

Let's not forget raise a glass for therapy,
And as we make a heartfelt toast...
Let us not forget to give thanks,
For all of life's blessings...
Including another day alive.

Human

Skin,
Bone,
And muscle-
We are human.
Lend a hand,
To someone in need.
Words and actions,
Impact the world.
We are human,
And need-
To be kinder.
How do you,
Want to be remembered?
My fellow human,
And friend...
Go out-
Make your mark.

Skin

No matter the color,
Of our skin-
We are human.
Race,
Doesn't define us.
What matters,
Is how we treat others.
Skin is skin,
Hearts beating-
We're human.
Love others,
Start a domino affect.
Hand in hand,
Making a change-
Go out,
Make your mark!

Popularity

Life isn't about popularity,
You were born to change-
The world.
We put on labels,
But we're all human.
Why try to hide,
When we're meant to be found.
Life isn't a contest.
Why fit in,
When born to be different?
Be yourself-
Go out,
Make your mark!

Beauty

Beauty-
Is more than skin,
It's who YOU are.
Looks catch the eye-
But beauty is more,
Than what eyes grasp.
Go further,
Than skin deep.
True beauty,
Lasts forever-
Never fading.
Day by day,
You blossom and grow.
Beauty is determined,
By mind and by heart.

Whisper

The wind,
Howling and crisp-
You make,
Your move.
The whisper,
Of wind-
Quiet,
But loud.
My ear strains,
To listen-
What did you say?
The whisper,
Of the wind-
Is but a mystery to me.
The whisper,
Tells a story.
What will yours be?
Whisper it,
Then live it.
Go out-
Make your mark.

The Future

Make the future bright,
With goals in sight.
Planning and working-
For the future.
Live in the now-
Reflect and learn,
From the past.
Prepare,
For the future,
Without hesitation.
The next day,
Is not promised.
Make the most-
Out of today!

Health

What does health mean to you?
Raise awareness-
For physical and mental health,
Impact the world.
We each have a story-
A mark being made,
To leave a legacy.
Look closely-
The smiles you see,
Can cry for help.
Eyes tell stories,
Of the soul's journey.

Cancer

This river of a bloodstream,
Carries my red blood cells . . .
To where they need to be.
A flood of white,
Comes to save the day.
The white blood cells,
Make me fight any infection . . .
That may come my way.
My platelets assist in the healing process,
When cuts or similar things arrive.

Life isn't perfect,
For all of us are bound to get sick . . .
In some way shape or form.

With cancer,
Certain cells uncontrollably separate.
When this happens . . .
Body tissues get destroyed.
Cancer comes in the form,
Of numerous amounts of names.
Chemo helps us fight the cancer,
But it doesn't always work.
Cancer is serious,
And we need a cure . . .
For it takes so many innocent lives.
Some people win their battle,
While some people pass away while fighting.

Stay strong butterfly,
You'll forever be loved.

A Letter to Cancer

Dear Cancer,

Please stop hurting me- I have a family.
You may be one of many,
That see no value in me- wanting me dead...
But please I beg you, spare my little head.

Please STOP hurting me…

Just cause you don't want me here,
Doesn't mean- Someone wouldn't miss me...
When my absence is noticed,
After time has passed.

Please stop hurting me- I have dreams.
If my life is cut short thanks to you,
Then I wouldn't be able to-
Cross everything off my bucket list...
Saying all my goals were met,
Like receiving my dream job...
Or becoming a mother,
The list is quite long...
So please I beg you, spare my little head.

Please STOP hurting me…

Why would you want to rob,
A woman of her hopes and dreams...
Especially when life practically just began?
That's just pure insanity,
But then again you don't care.

I'll ask again- only a little louder this time...

PLEASE STOP HURTING ME CANCER!!

If you end up succeeding in taking my life,
Instead of sparing my little head...
Like I have begged you to,
Then please at least let me...
Die in comfort and peace,
Instead of misery.

You're having your fun and games,
With my body- which belongs to the Lord...
But when my time does come,
You'll end up apologizing...
For the agony you put me through,
When you begin to see...
That walking in Heaven with the Lord,
Is truly the best place to be.

Please STOP hurting me...
I'll be eternally grateful.

Life Lessons from Cancer

Cancer does more than harm,
The Person it attacks…
It offers lessons in the midst of Pain.

A reminder from cancer,
Is to show and tell…
Those that are important to you,
How you truly feel…
Before it's too late.

One of the hardest lessons,
That cancer teaches…
Is that fighting to survive,
Will be incredibly difficult…
Since there isn't a cure.

The easiest lesson taught,
Is that Pausing every now and then…
To simply breathe while counting blessings,
Is often needed more than most realize…
Since they're usually in a rush.

Cancer does more than harm,
The Person it attacks…
It offers lessons in the midst of Pain.

If You or A Loved one,
Has been impacted by cancer…
Share this poem with them,
But make sure to include…
A note of your own,
So they'll forever remember…
They're loved—for you're cheering them on.

The Cancer Free Bell

Patients just want to ring the Cancer Free bell,

But Cancer tries to limit numbers of people…

For it wants to take innocent lives,

Even though it hurts their friends and family.

Cancer is one cruel fella - so to all the fighters,

I want to encourage you…

We'll all get through this together,

No matter what issues we may face…

So hold my hand dear friend,

You'll never face this alone-

And we WILL ring that bell!

Miracles

The train of pain came everyday,
Letting her see the rain...
That only angels see.

Over the years,
Her tears watered her fears...
Leaving her breathless,
In hopes for a miracle.

The world isn't as dark as it seems,
The woman's heart...
Just needs to remember,
That God is always working...
And with him in control,
Everything will be alright...
No matter how much time,
Seems to pass by.

Kaleidoscope of Mystery

Looking through a kaleidoscope,
The woman begins to see...
All the possibilities,
That the future holds.

It reminds her that the world,
Isn't all black and white...
And that with the Lord by her side,
Anything is possible.

With the sound of the waves,
Crashing in the distance...
The woman looks down,
At the sand beneath her feet.

The beach reminds her,
Of the past, present, and future...
Because the woman treated,
Life like a grain of sand.

To her life was a grain of sand,
Because in a flash it could be gone...
While each memory made,
Can last well over a lifetime.

Finding Stability

The past is a train station,
That we all eventually leave...
But need to learn from.

Just like the present,
Is a gift for you and me...
That we need to treasure.

While the future is unseen,
Holding great beauty....
That we mustn't try to erase.

Life may be unpredictable,
But that doesn't mean...
That everything's unstable.

If people opened their eyes,
Spending less time in front of screens...
We'd all begin to see,
How wonderful life can be...
Finally finding stability,
And a place to belong.

Your genuine smile is the only thing that will truly be able to complete your outfit.

Wearing makeup is fine, and not wearing makeup is also fine. PLEASE know that you ARE beautiful with or without makeup!

Reflect on life and remember that your words and actions impact or leave a mark on the world. If we want to see change in the world, we must start the change ourselves, so that way others will be inspired to change this cruel world into a peaceful one. It is more than true that one person can change the world!

Part Two

Being Different

Things to think about

Who are you? What will you do to be the best person you can be? Everyone in this world is different, and that's a good thing. If we were all the same inside and out, then the world would be quite boring. We as people were truly born to stand out, and not blend in. You can try to blend in with the crowd, but no one will be able to replace you. No matter who you are, your words and actions impact others and the world around you. What mark or impact do want you leave on the world?

Figuring out what's right and wrong can sometimes be difficult. The right thing is not always easy, but we must find the courage to do it. Doing the wrong thing might be easy, but we must focus on trying to do what's right. Being kind is something that this world will always need more of, and none of it will be wasted. When being kind or choosing what is right, you may not always see the results. If you are genuinely kind though, the world will thank you for it. Everyone you know is dealing with something, and certain things are harder than others. We must remember to extend a hand to others, no matter what's going on. It's easy to be selfish, and stick to ourselves, but it's important to help others. When helping others you can still ask for help, for all love is important.

The Peace in Prayer

When everyone around you,
Refuses to lean on the Lord…
It makes things so much harder,
Physically and emotionally.

The Heavenly Father wants his children,
To feel comfortable coming to him…
In any situation – good or bad,
For he loves them endlessly.

Praying about life's events,
Past, present, and future…
Is the greatest form of peace,
That'll ever be found…
For the Lord would never (ever),
Let his children drown…
Especially when they allow him,
To help them by letting him in.

Life will always be full of craziness,
Whether it be positive or negative…
Most of the answer depends,
On how the day to day events get handled…
And straying away from the Heavenly Father,
And straying away from the Heavenly Father,
Only ever leads to stress, pain, and heartbreak…
Which are all things that the enemy,
Really wishes to see happen.

Things handled with prayer and honesty,
Look extremely different…
Than anything handled with rash decisions,
And a happy or healthy heart…
Fully relies on allowing the good Lord,
To take control of life so he can lead…
This child of his that is in desperate need,
Of his guidance and a peaceful rest.

When the toxic people around you try to harm you,
Don't give them the satisfaction of having power over you…
For you belong to the Lord your God-
You are his creation,
Don't let them destroy who you are…
Because you are worthy of love and a beautiful life.

One Simple Request

Some people like sympathy and drama,
While others prefer honesty and loyalty.

If you can't keep it real with me,
Then what's the point...
Of even being near me.

If you're nothing but toxic,
I'll eventually cut you off...
For I have a life to live,
That I don't want spent in misery.

I give out chance after chance,
But I refuse to be a punching bag...
For anyone's pleasure.

All I ask is that you be honest and loyal,
Show me while you have me...
That you value having me near,
Or lose me forever...
With a zero chance,
Of ever finding me again.

Once I'm gone,
I'll be nowhere to be found...
So before you play me,
Make sure that your actions...
Show me how you feel,
Cause in my world...
Your actions are the echo,
To what your words really mean.

An Honest Word

If I give you my word…
You best believe that I'll keep it,
For I value honesty and trust.

One important thing...
That you should know about me-

Is that it's one of my biggest pet peeves,
When someone doesn't keep theirs...
For if a person doesn't mean something,
They shouldn't say it at all.

If I give you my word…
You best believe that I'll keep it,
For I value honesty and trust.

If you give me your word on something,
Please do us both a favor and mean it...
For I've been burned one to many times,
By people who ended up being toxic liars...
And I refuse to put up with hurtful people,
Since I know my worth in the Heavenly Father.

What Happened?

I was raised to believe,
That promises - of any kind...
Were not supposed to be broken.

For some unknown reason though,
A lot of the world doesn't see why...
Promises should be held or kept.

Whatever happened to honesty and trust?

This world that I live in scares me Lord,
And as you continue to...
Guide me on my journey,
I hope that more people will truly...
Allow you into their hearts.

If more people knew your grace,
It would make this broken world...
A much brighter and better place.

Whisking Away Drama

I’ve gotta drown out your bullshit and lies,
With several shots of whisky...
For I have zero time for drama,
I just want HONESTY.

Why is it so damn hard...
For people to be decent human beings,
Along with telling the truth?!?

I have no time for games,
So if that’s what you’re about...
Then please step away from me,
For I only want real people around me.

If you’re not happy,
Then please remember one thing...
To not make everyone around you,
Join you in your misery.

I understand asking for help,
But I’ll never understand...
Tearing someone down,
Just because life is tough.

I may not understand why,
You enjoy watching people suffer...
But I hope that one day,
You’ll allow the Heavenly Father...
To save and warm your cold cruel heart,
For he’s a good good Father.

As the days continue to go by,
I’ll be praying that one day,
You’ll see the light...
And finally understand why,
Being honest is so meaningful.

My Heart Cries Out

Does love exist?
My heart cries out.
Are your parents still together?
My heart cries out.
What was your home life like,
When growing up?
True love-
Is hard to find.
A heart can ache,
In the process.
My heart cries out.
Once true love-
Is found,
It is irreplaceable.
If you're not,
Truly in love-
The feeling of Melancholy,
Will take over.
My heart cries out.
Divorce?
Happily ever after?
A shattered heart,
Or a mended heart?
Hearts can be broken,
By anyone you're close with.
Family,
Friends,
Significant other-
But God will guide you.

Whether you're a broken window,
Or a window being repaired-
You are worthy.
Light your light,
Shine through darkness.
You will find love-
When you stop looking.
You can get through anything,
If you put your mind to it.
Let your heart cry out,
For help-
When needed.
You're not alone,
in the journey of life.
My hand is extended-
Hold on tight,
Don't let go.
My heart cries out for you.

Tears

Tears,
Rolling down my face.
Making room,
For happiness.
Rain and sun,
Needed-
To form a rainbow.
Life has ups and downs.
Tears,
Rolling down my face.
Go out,
Make your mark.
You could,
Be someone's rainbow.
Tears and smiles,
Memories will remain.

The Shepherd Knows Our Name

The world is full of Poisonous snakes,
People that want to watch you suffer…
Once your walls are torn down,
Leaving you vulnerable.

There are still honest and kind folks,
But they are very rare and hard to find…
They're almost becoming extinct,
Like an endangered species.

The Poisonous snakes usually take a while,
To come out of their shell…
Announcing their true agenda,
So please be careful - try to stay safe.

A lot of times though the snakes,
Tend to give us clues…
Like when they're extra greedy,
And we mustn't waste their clues…
Cut them off immediately,
This way they can't kill you too.

I know it can be hard to still be,
A gentle-loving soul…
In a cold and harsh world,
But Please do not let the snakes…
Take away one of the last few,
Beautiful things of this world.

When the end of time comes,
And the Lord calls us home…
We'll never have to deal,
With the snakes of the Past…
Since in Heaven - nothing gets past the Lord.
Which means we'll forever be safe…
We just have to trust and listen,
To the Shepherd that knows us by name.

The Bloody Assumption

Assumptions can be deadly.

When assuming something,
It's almost like getting blood…
On your hands that were,
Once actually clean.

Assumptions can be dangerous,
For they are usually wrong…
While being far from ever,
Having a chance of being correct.

If you want to find out something,
Take time to ask questions…
Instead of taking the lazy route,
Of just making assumptions.

You never know what battles,
Your neighbor may be fighting…
So lend a hand and help them,
You might just save their life.

One of life's biggest lessons,
Is to never make assumptions…

Assumptions can be deadly.

The Sleeve Remained Heartless

If you want to see through me,
Into my past and present…
Just use my poetry,
For it's like a crystal ball…
That will someday lead me,
Into the future…
Before the time comes,
For God to call me home…
My poetry will tell you,
The information that's needed…
Since the heart is something,
That doesn't belong…
On someone's sleeve,
Where it can get ripped to shreds…
For everyone's heart,
Needs protected from evil folks.

The Weekly Wish

As this week begins with a painful start,
I listen to the beat of the heart within me...

This week won't be able to go fast enough,
For it already feels like it's hardly moving...

With each minute that passes,
I faintly hear the clock ticking...
As the people around me whisper,
Extremely negative things in my ear.

As I wish for a place to belong,
I fall on my knees and begin to pray...
Hoping that the Lord will call me home soon,
For Earth isn't where I belong anymore.

The world is a harsh harsh place,
And when the time is right...
The the Heavenly Father,
Will reveal to us our consequences...
For every single action has repercussions,
Whether they be good or bad- is up to us.

This week seems to have no end,
For it feels like it has been way longer...
Than it actually has been.

Now that this week has come to an end,
It's time to repeat the process again...
And my weekly wish is that next weekend,
Will get here much quicker...
Than this one did.

The Lonely Days

When you spend almost every day alone,
It's fairly easy to waste the time sleeping.

When you spend almost every day alone,
It's fairly easy to feel replaceable.

When you spend almost everyday alone,
In a toxic household- it's fairly easy...
To hope one day soon you won't be breathing-
Unless there was an escape route somewhere,
That leads to someplace truly safe.

When you spend almost everyday alone,
It's easy for the mind to wander too far.

When you spend almost everyday alone,
Cries for help get buried or go unnoticed.

Spending almost everyday alone,
Is harmful to the heart and soul...
Which in turn makes the brain,
Frantically hunt for an escape...
To unwind or cry because,
Everyone needs someone to lean on.

Time alone is a good thing,
But only in smaller doses...

If you have to spend almost everyday alone,
I encourage you to pray and lean on the Lord...
For he'll help keep you sane,
Guiding you along the way.

The Heavenly Father will always,
Be there for you...
So please let him into your heart.

Dancing in RainStorms of Stardust

It's in the difficult times of life,
Where people's true colors...
Actually begin to show.

My heart has become an empty nest,
For it has been abandoned...
By people that claimed they cared.

A great deal of folks have forgotten,
That when words & actions don't match up...
Things get ugly extremely fast.

Being someone who had to grow up,
Faster than an average person would...
Has taught me a great deal of things.

I don't play with fire like the enemy does,
Instead I dance in the rainstorms of stardust...
While praying to my Heavenly Father.

My heart has become an empty nest,
For it has been abandoned...
By people that claimed they cared.

When I leave the world behind I'll be overjoyed,
Singin hallelujah- since walking with the Lord...
In Heaven is where I long to be.

Hurt

What is the meaning of strength?
What is the meaning of pain?
What will you do,
To get through-
This thing called life?
Everything in life happens,
Everyone you meet is there,
To teach you and to guide you.
Some lessons-
Are harder to learn,
Than the others.
It's okay to be hurt,
You will heal.
Darkness still has light,
So look to the stars.
Without struggle,
Strength is powerless.
Without being hurt,
Healing won't occur-
And neither will strength.
Without failing,
Success wouldn't be possible.
Life is full of ups and downs,
Make the most out of each day.
What mark will you leave,
When time is up?

Death Upon the Battlefield

Your mind is the battlefield,
Where your heart and soul…
Are at stake - for their death is near,
Since people tore down your walls…
Making you an easy target.

Anxiety and depression,
Are both so very real…
But the world only tries,
To sweep mental health under the rug…
Not caring who it may destroy,
For the world is a selfish place.

If you need a safe Place,
From the battle in your mind…
Or a break from the harsh world,
Take a seat next to me-
You'll never be alone…
This I promise you,
For the Lord sent me.

Depression

Being told to swim,
Forgetting how to-
Sinking.
Down,
Sinking-
Deeper in the water,
Almost reaching-
The bottom.
Maybe someone,
Will try to save you-
Extend your hand.
You're learning to walk,
Like a bird learns to fly.
It takes time to feel okay,
But,
Ask for help.
Trusting people,
Can be hard.
Don't let the darkness stay,
Let the light shine in.
Allow those that care,
To help.
You are worth fighting for.
Depression is a battle-
A battle that can be won,
Or one that takes precious lives,
Of people trying.
I'm extending my hand,
Out for you.
Hold on,
Let me help-
You're worth saving.

Fighting Death

Live life,
To the fullest.
Go out-
Make your mark.
Time is ticking,
Don't waste a moment.
Your every breath,
Means something.
Death will come,
Knocking-
At your door.
This isn't the end,
Keep fighting.
You haven't lost,
Have hope.
Shine your light-
Chase death away,
For a while longer.
It's not time to go yet-
You are loved,
You are cared for.
YOU MATTER.
No matter how hard,
Do not give up!
You can and will-
Get through this.
Live life-
To the fullest.
Life is short,
Do NOT make it shorter.
Life is full,
Of good times-
Of bad times,
And okay times.

A rainbow needs,
Sun and rain-
In order to arrive.
Don't lose hope now,
You've come this far.
You're fighting death,
Chasing it away-
With your ray of light.
Keep this hope,
For you are loved.
You are cared for.
You are wanted.
Go out-
Make your mark

Death

Drowning,
Suffocating-
Gasping for air.
Trying,
To hold on-
I can't do this.
Slipping away,
I don't belong.
Just end my pain-
I'm losing my fight,
With every passing day.
Stay strong?
Have hope?
It's all so hard.
What is life?
I'm just suffocating,
Grasping for air-
Help me hold on.
I'll stay,
Only for you.
I'll try,
To win this fight.
The fight against death-
Horrifying,
But shine your light.
Your light,
Will beat darkness.
Take a deep breath,
You belong.
You MATTER.
Don't let death win,
Have hope-
You are cared about.
Treasure every breath,
You can breath now-
Hold on.

Too Tired to Go On

Everyone has used me,
As their punching bag...

I'm beyond tired.

I have things I need to do,
In order to live and succeed...

I'm beyond tired.

I wanna make my guardian angels,
Proud of me and the life I've lived...

I'm beyond tired.

What will happen next Heavenly Father?
Cause I don't know if I have the strength...

I'm beyond tired.

There Seems to Be No Escape

Is it a waste of time to even try,
Especially when the world...
Is completely against you,
And would rather see you dead?

God - Why does breathing,
Seem insignificant right now?

God - Why can't you,
Take me from the cruel Earth yet?

I know I have a purpose,
And that you have a plan...
But with all this suffering,
I just wanna go home.

Gone

Memories made,
While time flies-
Life fades fast.
Today is here,
Tomorrow is near,
But not promised.
Alive or dead,
Parts of us-
Are gone.
With every day,
We die a little.
When we're gone,
Memories remain,
With those we've touched.
Our presence is gone,
The mark we made-
Forever lingers.

Clouds

A cloud,
Blocking my view-
From the truth.

A storm,
Making me,
Drown.
Losing hope,
But-
Trying to hold on.

Clouds blocking-
The light.
Reach your hand out to me.
God,
Since you care-
You pull me up,
Out of the water.

Through all times,
You're there.
Your soldiers,
Going through,
Good and bad-
But they need to know
They are never alone.

Clouds,

Slowly move-
To let the light in.

You are there,
Every step-
Of the way.

The clouds,
Have disappeared-
For now.

Guide me,
Help me see the light.

Don't let-
Clouds,
Make it to dark.
I need you Lord,
For all of my days-
You have all of me.

A Rainbow Appears

Sun,
Rain,
Then what?
A rainbow-
Starts to show,
First it's dim,
Then it brightens.
It won't rain,
Forever.
It won't,
Always be sunny.
The rainbow,
Might take a while-
To show itself.
This is life.
Good times,
Difficult times.
Good times,
Are sunny days.
Difficult times,
Are rainy days.
Combined,
We see the rainbow-
Appreciate the good times,
Learn from the difficult times.
Remember-
Live life fully,
Never give up,
No matter what.
YOU MATTER!
Go out-
Make your mark.

The Holiday Season

It's the holiday season,
And all I wanna do...
Is find peace.

The world is a place,
That I'll never understand...
For it's a harsh melancholy land.

Will there be peace on Earth,
As it was promised?

I wish more people,
Would walk by faith...
Trusting the Lord,
And his word...
Instead of allowing,
The world to brainwash them.

The world is a place,
That I'll never understand...
For it's a harsh melancholy land.

The holiday season promises peace,
So if there's sadness in your heart...
Dig deep and find your reason to smile.

The Heaven and Earth Holiday

As we celebrate the holidays,
My heart wishes you were here...
For you made them complete,
With your laughter and cheer.

All the memories we've made,
Will forever live on...
For you may be in Heaven,
But your legacy forever lives on.

As we celebrate the holidays,
We light a candle in honor of you...
And all our loved ones,
Who were taken to soon.

You touched the hearts of many,
While you were here on Earth...
And so many of us still want,
To say thank you for everything.

As we celebrate the holidays,
It still doesn't feel right...
Without you here - but we must,
Remember you're in a better place.

Dreams and Wishes

Dream a dream,
Make a wish.
With hard work-
The dream,
And wish,
Will become reality.
Hard works pays off-
Dream a dream,
Make a wish.
Be hopeful,
Even when feeling-
Melancholy.
Learn from hard times!
Dreams and wishes,
Make them come true.

The Empty Room

I sit inside this empty room.
Sitting inside this dark empty room,
I'm with a heartbreaking silence-
Wanting to go home.
I sit inside this empty room,
My emotions were nothing-
The feeling of melancholy taking over.

I closed my eyes,
Taking the breath…
The breath that I thought would be my last.

Then I opened my eyes and I saw you,
Standing right in front of me!
The breath I thought would be my last,
Taught me to live-
For each breath that comes next,
Is never promised!

How did I not see you before?
How did I not know you were here?
Why did I not know of your presence till now?

Wait…

I think I know why.

I'm sorry I was drowning,
My view was blurred from what matters most.

Home isn't just a house,
Home is where your heart leads you.
Home is more than just a place.

God's given me your presence,
You're a lifesaver.
I hold you near…

Life is more than what happened,
Life is more than what happens,
Life is more than what will happen...
Life is more.

The room may be empty,
Or seem dark for a while-
But if you truly open your eyes,
The room will be full…
I repeat,
The room will be full!

Tired of Trying

At this point I don't know why I try,
It always gets me nowhere...
Since almost everyone,
Is an imposter or fake.

I'm tired of people using me,
As a punching bag...
I'm tired of the Enemy,
Trying to drown me.

God - please help me,
In the good and bad...
For I'm tired of trying,
And just wanna go home.

God's Whisper

When you whispered my name,
It took away the aches and pains . . .
That my heart felt on a day to day basis.

When you whispered my name,
My glass of water . . .
Turned into wine.

When you whispered my name,
I finally began to breathe…
For the enemy tried to drown me.

When you whispered my name,
I was made new and set free . . .
Now I'll forever worship my Heavenly Father.

God Please

I'm alone.
And-
I'm tired.

I'm not sure...
How much fight,
Is left in me.

God please,
Call me home soon...
Before I lose my mind.

I'm tired.
And-
I'm alone.

The Reassuring Hug

Each hug from you,
The feel of your warm embrace...
Is like an Angel came down from Heaven,
To tell me - everything will be okay...
And to ask me - to not give up,
Reassuring me...
That I'll truly be glad I held on,
Instead of trying to escape from the world...
Allowing God to call me home naturally.

God Heals

Whether you believe in God,
Or whether you don't…
Know that you are loved.

There is a love so pure,
A love that's everlasting.
God's hand,
Is stretched out to you-
Ready to be taken.

Jesus walked on water,
And Jesus died so that we may live.
The cross is a reminder to be hopeful.

Life will be full…
Full of great times,
And full of melancholy feelings.

When drowning,
You won't sink-
God loves you and he's reaching out.

Even if things seem impossible to get through-
Look around you,
For someone is trying to help you.
You MATTER!!

There are angels on earth,
Sent by God to help those that are hurting-
Sometimes though,
It's the angels that are hurting.

Don't let the silence stay,
Help someone in need-
Even if you just simply smile their way from across the room.

God heals his people,
Just remember to always be kind-
You might just save someone's life.

Faded

Colors,
Fading into dark.
Eyes open,
Searching-
For light.
Feeling melancholy,
I'm faded.
The dark-
Overcame,
And faded the light.
Faded,
But not gone-
Hope will help,
Light life again.
Don't give up,
The light-
Is bright again.
YOU matter!

Stop and Go

Thinking,
Taking action-
Stop and Go.
Life's ups and downs,
Stopping to process-
Information.
Try to be,
Open minded,
And kind.
Go and make,
Your mark.
You'll not be forgotten!
Melancholy and joy,
Stop and Go-
You're precious,
So just do you!

Words and Actions

Words and actions,
Need to be met.
Be truthful,
But kind.
Words and actions,
Impact the world.
Negative,
Or positive,
All actions-
Change the world.
Chase away,
The melancholy feeling.
While memories,
Are being made,
Go out-
Make your mark!

The Sleep Schedule

As I sleep - dreams find me,
But occasionally...
Nightmares do too.

As I sleep - the things that come to me,
All mean something...
Even if I don't know what they're telling me.

As I sleep - my brain doesn't turn off,
It's on practically 24/7...
Unlike a light switch,
Where power and energy can be saved.

As I sleep - for a period of time,
My mind wanders...
Sometimes to places unknown.

As I sleep - my body knows,
That eventually it'll be time to awaken...
For since we're human we can't sleep forever.

School

Teachers,
Students-
All with classes.
Education,
Happens.
School,
Making memories-
For several years.
Graduation comes.
School helps,
With future plans.
Work,
And school-
Go hand in hand.
School may be tough,
But you will succeed.

Social Media

Followers, Likes,
Sharing, Reading,
Chatting-
Social media,
It's more than that.
The number of likes,
The number of followers,
Shouldn't matter.
Allow the people,
That love you for you,
To come and stay.
Be careful with social media.
Wonderful things,
And bad things,
Can happen-
Stay true,
To who you are.
Don't change,
So others will like you,
Just follow your heart.
Never underestimate,
The power-
Of words,
And actions.
Do your words and actions agree?
Go out,
Make your mark.
though,
Your mark,
Is your footprint on the world.
Whether you use social media,
Or whether you don't,
You will be remembered.
How do you want to be remembered?
Go out,
Make your mark.

Roads

Eyes open,
Traveling.
The dark road,
The light road,
All things happen-
For a reason.
The dark road-
Is a struggle that causes,
Melancholy feelings.
The light road-
Is a joyous love,
That's everlasting.
Some roads rougher-
Than others.
Always be kind!

Disasters

Every time I turn around,
Disasters happen.
Losing hope,
In humanity.
People take,
Kindness as weakness-
When it's really strength.
Disasters happen,
All the time.
Turn off the news,
For a while-
Explore,
See the world,
It isn't that scary.
Every time the news is on,
We as people see-
Disasters happen every day.

A Want and Need for Safety

I just want to feel emotionally safe,
Is that too much to ask for...
In a place of shelter?
A place of shelter shouldn't only,
Be safe for physical needs...
It should also be a place,
Where the heart and soul can rest...
Instead of having to wonder when,
The next attack will take place.

The heart, soul, and mind...
Go through enough each day,
Why is it so hard for people...
To genuinely be kind?
There's physical abuse and emotional abuse...
Both of which can be pretty scary.

If you have the honor of being,
In a home with people...
That actually want you around,
And care wholeheartedly...
About your safety and well being,
Then please count your blessings twice...
For you're richer than some of us.

Some of us are stuck with people,
Who are sadly two faced...
Which means in public,
They deserve the #1 whatever award...
But when away from crowds or other folks,
It all goes back to normal...
Where we are either reminded,
With words or with actions...
That we aren't truly wanted,
And most of us in this situation...
Hate burdening people.

Heavenly Father... please hear the cry,
For physical safety AND emotional safety-
They both have great importance,
In each child or adults life...
And they shouldn't be robbed of that.

The world is a cold cold place,
Since not everyone knows your grace...
Please help your children Lord,
We need you now more than ever.
I love you with my heart, soul, and mind Lord,
And even though I'm one who may not...
Be in a house that's fully safe,
I hope you'll hear my cry for help...
And guide me to someplace safer,
One where I won't have to hide.

Abandoned

Lost and alone,
Almost forgotten-
I'm abandoned.
Searching,
For light-
Calling,
For help.
Abandoned,
But brave-
Getting through,
The night.
A hand,
Is stretched out-
To save me.
No longer,
Abandoned.
Light is found-
Always have hope,
No matter what!

Shattered

Hearts breaking,
More and more-
every day.
Shattered hearts,
Losing hope.
Darkness,
Takes over-
For a while.
Light will find,
It's way back.
Shattered and broken,
Trying to have hope-
Seems impossible,
Till you fully believe,
Miracles can happen.

I'll be Waiting for You

What did I do wrong,
To make you want to delete me...
Right after you created me?
Would having a child be that horrible?
Why don't you want me?
What can I do to make you see value in me?

I'd really like a chance,
To blossom and grow...
And someday hear your voice.
It's the little things,
That make me excited...
For I know the Lord is good.

I hope you understand,
That if you go through with this...
I'll feel every ounce of pain just like you.

I know that this is your body,
And I'm technically intruding...
But why would you,
Do something to create me...
If you didn't possibly want,
A miniature version of you...
Someday running around?

I don't understand- but I want to,
So please help me understand why you say...
That abortion is the only way to go.
Then again if you go through with everything,
I'll get to walk by the Lord's side forever...
Not having to worry about the world's dangers.
If you go through this heartbreaking thing,
I hope you're able to comprehend...
That many people will be upset.

If you go through with this,
I hope that you know I love you so much...
Even though you cut my life too short,
Not even allowing me one moment...
That's out of the womb.

This poem that was created for you,
Was NOT meant as an attack...
So please don't see it that way.
This poem is simply a reminder,
That I'll be waiting in Heaven for you...
If you succeed in sending me away.

It’s Okay to Cry

Infants cry.
Children cry.
Teens cry.
Adults cry.

We as people,
Have tears to let out...
So we all must cry,
At some point in our lives.

Yes some of us cry more than others,
But that’s okay because you and I...
We’re both human with feelings,
And keeping them bottled up...
Can be a dangerous thing,
So don’t be afraid to feel.

We as people,
Have tears to let out...
So we all must cry,
At some point in our lives...
But we also need to remember,
That once the tears pass...
There will be room,
For another smile.

The world is a harsh place,
Sometimes making it feel...
Like there’s no place safe,
But if we open our hearts...
To the Lord up above,
We’ll never have to face...
A single day alone,
For he’ll always be with us...
In the valleys,
Along with the mountains.

Why?

I once was a little girl,
Then I started to grow up.
Never knowing when,
I'd see you again-
You broke my heart first.

I've blamed myself before,
For not being good enough.
I thought that if I was enough-
I wouldn't have to wonder,
When I'd see or hear from you.

Dad I've cried tears for you,
Asking Jesus-
Why I couldn't see you.

Growing up I never knew when,
I'd see you face,
Or hear your voice again.
I still don't know why…

I once was a little girl,
Then I started to grow up.
Never knowing when,
I'd see you again-
You broke my heart first.

Dad I've cried tears for you,
Asking Jesus-
Why I couldn't see you.

Jesus healed my heart,
When I finally gave my all to him-
He's helped me see,
Through all the rain.

I know you're not perfect,
I forgive you for all your mistakes-
I love you as you are dad.

Forgive me for not being,
A perfect daughter, sister, or friend-
But I'm doing my best to show my love.
I hope one day I'll make you proud,
By being the daughter-
That you've always wanted.

I once was a little girl,
Now I've finally grow up.
I still don't know when,
I'll see you again-
But dad please know,
I love you and our family.

Forgiveness

Forgiveness is powerful.
Forgiveness,
Spreads peace.
Don’t hold grudges,
Spreading-
Melancholy feelings.
Be kind and hopeful,
Make your mark-
On the world.
Forgiveness is healing.
Forgive all people,
You truly matter!
Forgiveness is powerful.

Peace

Always be kind,
You might save-
Someone's life.
Stay true,
To you.
Work hard,
To put peace-
In the world.
Heartache
Can last a while,
So can happiness.
With hope,
And peace-
Life will be joyous.
Don't let,
Melancholy feelings-
Take over.
Spread peace!

The Girl Who Grew Up too Fast

I may currently be a woman,
But I once was a little girl...

I need to slow down for a moment,
And say dear younger me...
For it'll make me reflect,
On everything I've gone through...
And it may even help this woman,
Who's no longer so young...
Continue to grow and find her true potential.

I may currently be a woman,
But I once was a little girl...

To the little girl that once was,
There's a few things we need to discuss,
This way when the future comes...
Things may not be so difficult on our journey.

Advice is a tricky thing,
But one thing I know for sure...
Is that giving up on your dreams,
Should never be thought about.

Another piece of advice I'd like to offer,
Is that when toxic people try to kill you with hatred...
Cut them off quickly faster than you can blink,
For your safety and happiness...
Are more important than you think.

Young girl of the past I need you to know,
That it's okay you fell apart so many times...
And that you've had to grow up faster than most,
But the important part is,
Each time you got back up while seeking the Lord.

Our journey will be similar for I'm telling you all this,
As I'm a grown woman looking back at our history...
Because it's once again time to prepare for the future,
That God has planned for you and for me.

I may currently be a woman,
But I once was a little girl...
And no matter how much time seems to pass by,
The past and the present will always go hand in hand.

Age won't stop the Heavenly Father from lighting the way,
For his plans are greater than yours or mine,
So dear younger me...
Rest easy and smile sunshine it'll all be alright.

The Elderly Woman

I once was a little girl,
Who's currently a young woman...
That will one day become elderly.

In the past I've reflected on my history,
Giving younger me some advice...
This way the woman I was,
Could continue to grow.
The past and the present both play vital roles,
When it comes to preparing for the future that lies ahead.

I'm currently a young woman,
Who will one day become elderly...
But before I age much more I must write a letter,
To the elderly version of me this way I'll have a keepsake...
That will remind me of my journey,
While helping me prepare...
For going home to the Heavenly Father,
When this heart of mine decides to stop.

I once was a little girl,
Who's currently a young woman...
That will one day become elderly.
Dear older me,
As you begin to read this I hope you understand...
That the little girl you used to be was loved dearly,
And so was the young woman whose place you have taken recently.

The little girl you used to be had to grow up too fast...
But you made it through everything,
Because you trusted the Lord's plan.
The young woman you used to be face challenges,
Like the little girl you used to be...

But she as well overcame what was sent to destroy her,
Because she trusted that Lord would never abandon her...
In the valleys or the mountains.
Dear older me,
As you wait to go home...
To Father in Heaven,
I need you to know a couple things.

The biggest thing you must know,
Is that your life was lived to the fullest...
And that you've helped way more people,
Than one singular person...
So you completed the job,
That you had wanted to all those years ago.

The final thing you must know is that now that the end is near,
When God calls you home you'll be deeply missed...
By everyone who knew you,
But your mark will forever live on.

The little girl that you used to be,
Along with the young woman you used to be...
Are forever thankful for being apart of the life you have lived...
And they both wish to say thank you,
For making life so beautiful.

Precious Flower

You are a flower,
Growing and living.
Don’t let-
Someone pick you,
Just for their enjoyment.
Stick to your roots,
Be you.

A Change of Scenery

Being stuck under a shoe,
Is far from being fun...

As I look for the sun I begin to realize,
That I won't have much luck...
For I jeopardized that,
When I wished for world peace.

Being stuck under a shoe is the way it feels,
When the world around you,
Tells you that your dreams...
Won't come true because of who you are.

Being stuck under a shoe,
Is far from being fun...

As I look for a way to better myself,
I struggle underneath the pressure...
That the world's giant shoe,
Puts on my heart, soul, and mind.

Being stuck under a shoe,
May cause pressure and pain...
But each tear and moment of struggle,
Teaches me that I'm stronger than I know.

With each battle I've faced I've made it through alive,
So as I live this brand new day I must remember to thank...
The Lord up above who pulled me out,
From underneath the world's giant shoe.

When the Heavenly Father took me into his arms,
He allowed me to sit in a tree telling me I'm free...
No longer a slave to the cold cold world.

As I sat in the tree pondering,
Everything that could be...
The Lord was still right beside me,
Reassuring me that he'd always be with me.

The worlds giant shoe of melancholy,
And the Lord's tree of peace...
Are vastly different,
And if you want to join me...
Where we can see butterflies,
While hearing our guardian angels sing...
And if you're looking for an everlasting love,
I recommend sitting on the tree of peace...
Allowing the one who created you,
To come into your heart and stay.

The Woman and the Rainbow

The colors of the rainbow,
Are found in every corner...
For the woman within me,
Has found them on her journey.

The rainbow shared its colors,
With the woman...
Because it felt she shouldn't be alone,
In anyway shape or form.

The woman's favorite color blue,
Tasted like a sea of sadness...
But it also tasted,
Like a glimmer of hope.

This was because,
The rainbow had a lesson to teach...
A hard headed woman,
And it wouldn't be easy.

The rainbow was kind,
While most of the world...
Was full of hate,
And the rainbow wanted...
The woman to not be afraid,
Of who the Lord called her to be.

The woman's favorite color blue,
Tasted like a sea of sadness...
But it also tasted,
Like a glimmer of hope...
Because the rainbow needed,
The woman to understand...
That life may be tough,
But it's vital to never give up.

With the rainbow by her side,
The woman began to see...

The definition of true beauty,
Because she finally stopped seeking,
The approval of those around her...
And focused on the opinion,
Of her one true king in heaven.

The Woman In The Woods

Hurt from within,
A lady begins to hunt...
For a place to belong,
Someplace she won't have to hide.

Tired of crying,
Tired of trying...
The woman keeps fighting,
Even now that her strength...
Has started to vanish,
Right into thin air.

Woods surround the woman,
And they tell her...
That everything will be okay,
For they've protected her...
From sun and rain for so long,
That they now know...
Which footsteps belong to her,
Because the Lord commanded them...
To give her shelter,
From the harsh harsh world.

Whether things are clear,
Or hard to see...
The woman in the woods,
Has much to teach you and me...
For we need to learn to walk by faith,
And trust God's timing...
For he's fighting our battles,
Even when it feels like he's absent.

The Lord's Gift

Having a cup of tea or coffee,
With a loved one used to be common...
But nowadays it seems,
Like everyone's on their phones.

Enjoying the weather outside,
Used to be popular...
Until electronics started taking over,
And controlling more people.

Electronics may have become popular,
But money will always be number one...
On a lot of people's list,
Of things they want an endless supply of.

Money is a crazy thing,
For it makes so many people...
Become greedier by the minute,
Instead of being thankful...
For what they have,
Because the good Lord blessed them.

If money were to grow on trees,
It would be a sight to see...
But it's a good thing that it doesn't,
Because then the world...
Would have another reason,
To have more violence.

When money is involved,
Wonderful things can be bought...
And needs can be met,
But there's only one problem...
And it's the fact that when money's involved,
Thieves come out of the woodwork...
Making those less fortunate,
Suffer in more ways than one.

As we the people continue our journey,
There are several questions...
We need to ask ourselves individually,
A few for example are:
Am I being the best person I can be?
How would I feel if I was treated this way?
What impact am I leaving on others?
How do I want to be remembered?

As today comes to a close,
And we the people prepare for tomorrow...
We need to remember,
That today was a gift from the Lord...
And that we should give him thanks,
Before we head to sleep.

The Teaching Season

The seasons of the world,
Have shown the woman...

What warmth feels like,
And...
What cold feels like.
The warmth and the cold,
Taught the woman...
That she must always be careful,
For the world isn't always...
As safe as we'd like it to be.

The enemy finds,
The Children of God valuable...
But the thief of peace...
Won't win the war he tries to start,
For Lord never abandons his people.

The cold seasons,
Have given the woman a chance...
To experience snow, ice, and frostbite,
Along with so much more.
The warm seasons,
Have given the woman a chance...
To experience sun, rain, and flowers blooming,
Along with so much more.

Spring, summer, fall, and winter,
Have all been a teacher...
For a woman who was dying,
Trying to give her hope...
For whatever time she may have had left,
Before going home to Heaven...
And becoming one with the seasons.

As people we can all learn from this woman,
After all we're all dying slowly but surly...
And we never know when time will be up.

The day after today is far from promised,
So we the people need to make sure...
That the life that we're living,
Is to the fullest without regrets...
Because the woman of the seasons,
Would only want what's best for us.

The Enemy's Tricks

I've been avoiding the mirror of tears- my reflection,

For there'd be nothing but fears and scars...

So instead of looking where the enemy wants me to,

I've been out in the field with the sun, moon, and stars...

Hiding from the enemy and his tricks,

Praying that the Lord calls me to join him...

Sooner rather than later,

But until then I'll be wearing the armor of God...

Telling the devil to back off- leave me alone,

For I'm a child of the One True King...

And I won't let him freeze my heart into stone,

I may not know the good Lord's plan for me...

But I do know he'd never abandon me.

Surviving

This cold hearted world,
Has its hands...
Tightly against the woman's throat.

All she wants to do is breath,
But the world keeps trying...
To tell her who to be.

The world is an abusive place,
Where it's hard to stay alive...

Self abuse,
Abuse from others,
The cycle is endless.

Is it so wrong to just want to belong?

Is it so wrong to not want to feel,
Like a burden to others?

This cold hearted world,
Has its hands...
Tightly against the woman's throat,
But the Heavenly Father holds her...
Telling her everything will be okay,
Even if it feels like it won't be.

The woman thinks,
One day I'll be truly free...
For the Lord will have called me home,
To where I truly belong...
Which is away from this place called Earth,
That so many people seem infatuated with.

It'll be good to someday go home,
To the one true King...
But until then,
I'll do what I can to survive this thing called life.

The Enemy's Lies

The devil's tongue,
Is cruel and twisted...

For it'll try to convince,
The children of God...
That they're worthless,
And unloveable.

It'll try to persuade,
The children of God...
That if their father loved them,
They wouldn't be in pain.

Satan's tongue is twisted,
Full of nothing but lies - so ignore him.

The Never Ending Tug of War

The Enemy tries to quiet my singin voice,
And tries to completely defeat me...
For he wants me to blame the Lord,
While giving up on this thing called life.

The Enemy and the Lord both know me,
But I have the right to choose...
Whom I listen to giving them power.

The Heavenly Father is fighting,
All of my battles while holding my hand...
BUT the Enemy tries to make me believe,
That I'm alone in this fight.

It's a never ended tug of war game,
Because God wants to see me flourish...
While the Enemy wants to see me die.

The Enemy tries to quiet my singin voice,
For he knows that if I trust God...
Then I'll have all the strength I need,
To live the best life possible...
Never giving Satan the satisfaction,
Of destroying a child of the one true King.

Silencing the Storm

Anxiety can strike at any time,
For it doesn't care if you're here or there...
At home or out and about.

Anxiety is more than feeling anxious,
Anxiety is more than piled on stress...
Anxiety is more complicated than it seems.

Anxiety doesn't care who's around,
It'll attack when it wants to...
And it's not always controllable.

Anxiety attacks are far from fun,
In fact they're serious...
And should never be joked about.

If anxiety attacks tend to be frequent,
It's important to pay attention...
To what triggers them and helps calm them.

Anxiety attacks are like a storm,
For they're not always able to be seen...
At least until they strike.

Anxiety attacks are storms that are formed,
In the mind, heart, and soul...
Which is why they're so intense.

Anxiety can be hard to silence-
At times it can almost be impossible...
To quiet the storm of anxiety.

With the right people around,
And faith in the Heavenly Father,
You'll be able to get through anything...
Including anxiety-
So don't get discouraged,
Keep your head up precious butterfly...
Soar across the sky with your hopes held high.

The Silenced Woman

The feeling of wanting to belong,
Was strong in the woman's heart...
But day after day and night after night,
The world kept telling her to be quiet.

The hateful comments would tell her,
Your voice is insignificant...
Which is why we want you quiet,
This way your breath isn't wasted.

You're far from being one of us,
So why begin to try?

You're human like the rest of us,
But you're far from ordinary...
Which scares a lot folks,
And the government doesn't want that.

Tear after tear the woman cried,
While down on her knees...

What did I do wrong?
Why does everyone hate me?
Would anyone even miss me,
If I vanished into thin air?
Would anyone even notice,
That I was gone and nowhere to be found?

Lord help me understand why,
Everyone's being so cruel...
For I don't know how much more,
My heart will be able to handle.

I want your will to be done,
But with the world trying to keep me muted...
It's hard to make a difference,
Positive or negative.
Heavenly Father I ask of you,
Help me find my voice...

So I can face my attackers,
In the full armor of your glory...
For without you in my valleys or mountains,
I'd already be dead and gone...
Which is what the enemy wants,
And I'm thankful you won't let him win...
Any of the wars or battles,
That he tries to start and finish.

Silenced by A Mocker

I sit across from you silently,
As you continue to mock me...
I would speak - but it would be pointless,
Since you only care about yourself.

Never Understanding Why

I'll never understand why you hide,
Your pain behind your hands...
But then again that's fair-
For you'll never understand why,
I hide my pain in my poetry...
For when face to face,
I've revealed my pain…
I've been burned severely,
Way too many times.

The Exhausting Lifestyle

All of these aces and pains,
Just won't go away...
And you're trying to see me,
But you're failing miserably...
For these times we live in,
Are very restricting...
Which is making existing,
Even more exhausting.

Refreshing Poetry

Poetry is cleansing for the soul,
And it's the detox your heart needs...
While it's the minds therapy,
When the cold world is bossy...
So don't be afraid to pick up your pen,
For writing poetry can be refreshing.

Buried Alive

When you can't get the hug you need,
Bury yourself in some poetry...
You may not fully feel better- from crying & writing,
But it'll help letting everything out.

Forever Hiding

When you hide tears - through running water,
You truly know... you've hit an all time low.

The Sorrow in Giving Up

Poetry comes and goes,
With life's highs and the lows...

Life likes to keep us on our toes-
Which sometimes gets fairly old...

The battles faced each day,
May not end in a hooray...

Which means we mustn't give up in sorrow,
For our greatest adventure may be tomorrow.

The Fight of a Lifetime

When you feel like a waste of space,
It's hard to not leave without a trace...

Then from around the corner,
Someone came walking into your life...
Showing you that you that you matter,
Even when the toxic people said otherwise...

Which makes you stop planning an escape,
From th is cold cruel world...

And ends up giving you a reason,
Meaningful enough - to fight for your life.

A Woman with Baby Fever

When you can't have a child,
Of your own quite yet...
It can be rather difficult,
To not be a little sad.

Especially...

If everyone around you,
Seems to have children...
Making your baby fever grow,
Even though you know...
That it wouldn't be good,
To have a child right now.

When you can't have a child,
Of your own quite yet...
It can be easy to get impatient,
Wanting time and healing to go faster.

As a woman of God,
It may be hard to wait...
To have a child of my own,
But I must trust the Lord's plan.

Everyone Needs a Home

Being a biological parent,
Is a beautiful thing.

Being a God Parent,
Is a beautiful thing.

Being an adoptive Parent,
Is a beautiful thing.

Being a foster Parent,
Is a beautiful thing.

Being a fur mom or dad,
Is a beautiful thing.

If you're a parent in any way,
I just want you to know…
That I'm proud of you,
For I know parenting is far from easy.

The Poet's Feelings

Poets and misery,
Go hand in hand...
For you rarely see,
Poets that are happy.

The happy poets remember,
To count each blessing...
More than once,
For they remember...
Their heartbreaking past.

The poets that are miserable,
Will one day be happy...
But each trial they face now,
Will make the good days...
Even more enjoyable,
And even memorable.

Everyone has a mark to leave,
What will yours be?

The Poet's Canvas

There's no control over a poet's pen,
For the heart spills out...
Melancholy feelings,
Along with Anger...
Sadness and,
Anything else that's felt.

Paper is a canvas,
For the heart and soul...
For they go through so much,
Most of which isn't asked for.

As life's journey continues,
There's so much...
To be thankful for,
Even if...
The blessings that were given,
Seem to be harder to find.

When the poems you read,
Seem concerning in some way...
Just remember that the heart,
Bleeds out ink telling the poets story.

The Poet Critic

I've written some poetry,
That I'm not quite proud of...

Then again since I'm a poet,
Emotions and words...
Hit the page,
Even when I'm not thinking.

Whether I'm happy or sad,
Whether I'm mad or hurt...
No matter what the feeling is,
If my heart feels compelled by life...
It spills itself on the page,
Through thick black ink.

I've written some poetry,
That I'm not quite proud of...

Not all of my pieces of poetry,
Will get shared with another set of eyes...
For some of it deserves to be burned,
For it's either that harsh or poorly written.

I know that there's a saying,
About everyone being their own worst critic...
But this isn't me being hard on myself,
For there really are poems of mine...
That I'll never be proud of.

Art From the Heart

Poetry is art from the heart...
Each verse is never rehearsed,
For the feelings that are felt...
Are what the pen stains on the page.

Poetry is art from the heart...
For the heart and soul,
Are put through so much...
During life's roller coaster ride,
Of ups and downs.

Poetry is art from the heart...
That will never be able to be erased,
For people don't always...
Forget what they've been through.

Faith and Religion

Everyone tries to throw a label,
On who I truly am...
What they don't understand,
Is that's not how it works...
Because there's a major difference,
Between religion and faith.

There's all kinds of religions,
And I respect them all...
But I hope those that meet me,
Realize that I'm not a religion...
And that I walk by faith,
Because I'm a disciple...
Of a wonderful king,
Who has given me life...
While refusing,
To ever give up on me.

When faith becomes religion based,
That's when things get scary...
Because if we walked by religion,
Then faith along with the trust that was built...
Can easily disappear,
Because things become harder to see...
When it's important to know that with faith,
No matter how difficult...
Or unbearable life tries to get,
Things will always workout in the end.

Faith and Religion,
Are very different things...
And if more people,
Started walking by faith...
Instead of constantly,
Trying to label everyone by religion...
The world would be,
A much brighter place.

The World

Everyone and everything,
Is part of the worlds painting.
Each of us,
Adding vibrant and dark colors-
To the masterpiece.
With Known and unknown,
Vibrant dark colors-
Remember all are unique.
Open your eyes-
Make today,
A great day in the world.

Home

The USA was born.
It made a vow to be good,
Even when the air felt cold, the promise was kept.
Erie people and others arrived;
People traveled from afar to the good old USA.
Suddenly I heard a bang-
I ran,
There was war;
I feel sick.
Will I die?
What will happen?
My life was flashing, before my eyes-
I saw a flame lit off in the distance,
Switch gears-
Whether it's your final moments or not-
Keep your head up
You're real and alive in this moment.
Persevere.
Stay strong.
Stay true to you.
You can and will get through this-
Life is too short,
To live with regrets.
Have hope always,
Now you're home.

Freedom

The freedom we have,
Isn't free.
The price-
For our freedoms,
Repeatedly getting paid.
Value each moment-
Learn from past experiences,
Live for today...
Prepare for futures unseen.
Make each moment count,
You're breathing and alive-
Always be thankful.

The Day I Lost You

You're in Heaven now,
But losing you was beyond hard...

Watching you in your final days,
Was absolutely brutal...
But I wouldn't trade a second,
Of our final days for the world...
Because each moment with you,
Will forever be treasured.

Watching you pass on,
Wasn't an easy thing to do...
But I guess that's how it was meant to be.

You're in Heaven now,
But losing you was beyond hard...

Watching a loved one pass away,
And gain their Angel wings...
Can be hard to fathom,
Because we don't want to imagine...
A world without that person,
But we must be strong...
And remember they'll always be with us.

Whether it be in a hospital room,
Or whether it be at home...
Watching loved ones pass on,
Like I watched you...
Is part of the reason why,
Rivers... lakes... and oceans...
Or any body of water for that matter,
All have so much H_20...
Sometimes causing floods.

I'm trying to keep your legacy alive,
But I wish you hadn't gone so soon...
For I wanted more time with you.

You're in Heaven now,
But losing you was beyond hard...
And I hope that one day, I'll make you proud.

Grandfathers Never Truly Die

A grandfather's love,
Is worth more than gold.

A grandfather's love,
Is more special…
Than love from a stranger.

A grandfather's love,
Can be lifesaving…
So we mustn't forget,
To value every moment.

A grandfather's love,
Is more special…
Than any possible gift.

A grandfather's love,
Will never die-
Even if he moves to heaven…
For he'll find ways through God,
To show you he's forever with you.

A grandfather's love,
Is extremely special…
Since it's honest and real.

A grandfather's love is valuable,
In more ways than most understand.

A Love Forever Prayed For

I've always wanted your opinion on my poetry,
For the part of me that was gifted by you...
Has been printed in bold black ink,
For you'll forever be a part of me.

I may not understand why,
You left the world so soon...
But each sunrise and sunset,
Is completely different without you.

Whenever I look at the stars,
I realize that's where you are...
In Heaven watching over me,
But I still wish things ended differently.

Thank you for guiding me,
And for being my safe place...
You gave me the first home,
That I've ever known...
And most importantly,
You showed me what true love is.

My new and final home is in the arms,
Of my better half...
Who I really wish you could meet,
For you'd love him too...
He's honestly the man,
That you prayed I would someday find...
When the time was right - in God's eyes,
For he knows what's best for his people.

The Connection

Water flows,
Connecting to land.
Beating hearts,
Connecting to life.
Feel your heartbeat-
For no one,
Will ever replace you.
Make your mark-
Leave your footprint,
On the earth.
Even in dark times-
You are never alone,
For I'll always be with you.

The Hardest Words to Hear

Losing a loved one is never easy,
Whether you're a mother or father…
Brother, sister, grandparent, child, or friend,
It's beyond hard most times.

There are so many things,
That take loved ones away…
Whether it be old age,
Cancer or another disese…
No matter the reason,
It doesn't soften the blow…
When you hear the words,
I'm sorry for your loss.

Leaving earth is a part of life,
And I look forward to joining…
The Heavenly Father,
When he calls them home…
But I cherish my time alive,
No matter how difficult things are.

If you know the pain and heartbreaks
Of losing loved ones like I do…
Take my hand-know you're not alone,
For they'll always be with you…
No matter how hard it is to comprehend that,

Please remember…
You'll forever have a friend in me,
Since the Lord gifted us friendship.

Passing On A Legacy

They said her life was a story,
But they couldn't comprehend...
How she's held on for so long,
Without putting it to an end.

Traveling in time,
Through the pages of history...
The woman wanted one thing,
And that was to not be a burden.

When the woman looked back,
Her past guided her...
But for some reason,
She had a hard time...
Living in the moment,
Because the future wasn't far away.

As time passed and the woman aged,
She finally gained the knowledge...
That she needed to succeed,
But her battles weren't easy...
For everyone challenged her,
While some almost killed her with hatred.

Kindness was always around,
But it liked to hide in nooks and crannies...
Just like her loved ones promised,
Because they wanted her to know...
God gives his hardest battles,
To his strongest soldiers.

When the woman later passed on,
Her book was placed on a shelf...
And now it waits to be read,
Hopefully inspiring someone...
To not give up,
And live a life full of hope.

The Heavenly Reunion

No matter how much time goes by,
It'll always be difficult…
To know that you're no longer,
Here on Earth with me.

No matter how much time goes by,
I'll forever wish I could've said goodbye…
Giving you a proper farewell,
Other than the funeral.

No matter how much time goes by,
I'll never forget your hugs…
And everything you were,
After all, you were my hero.

I know I never said it enough,
While you were alive and well…
Before the Lord called you home,
But please know I love and miss you…

You'll remain in my heart-
Until the Heavenly Father calls us to reunite.

The Funeral

You left this earth,
To be in heaven.
You were an angel,
On earth-
Now you're home,
But will be missed.
The funeral,
Is heartbreaking-
But it's a chance,
To remember you,
Through memories.
You're watching over,
Those you loved-
You're finally at peace.
You'll always be,
In the hearts-
That were touched,
By your soul.
Death is not,
The end of your story.
For you left a mark,
On the world-
It will forever live on.

Goodbye

You left a mark-
On the world...
So sad you left-
But,
You will be remembered
Forever
Your memory will live on
All of us-
Had to move on...
I hated it-
Saying goodbye
So damn hard
You'll always be in my heart though
I guess I shouldn't cry-
I wish I didn't have to say it...
This it-
I love you,
Goodbye.

You may not always see the outcomes of your kindness, but they are helping turn this world into one that's great. Acts of kindness and respect are always appreciated!

What mark are you leaving on the world? Let's take a moment to appreciate all of the little things.

About the Author

Diana Douglas is from Kent, Ohio and loves working with children. She works with children all the time at church; and is going to college to become an Elementary school teacher and a counselor. Diana makes custom quilts (including t-shirt quilts). She attends craft shows in the fall and early winter every year selling things she has made or created. She has been sewing and quilting since she was really young because her grandmother taught her that homemade stuff will be treasured for a longer period of time. If something lacks the presence of the heart, more and more people will be quicker to turn away or throw something away. Whenever Diana picks up the pen, it's like a whole new world begins.

Made in the USA
Monee, IL
08 June 2023

35163519R00121